POLITRICKS:
It's all political

Matthew and James Dale

Copyright © 2021

POLITRICKS: It's all political

Matthew and James Dale

Cover design: James Dale

ISBN: (paperback) 9781980614609

For more information contact me here:

Eaton220@gmail.com

Please check out other books:

Just Another Hope-Full Fool in Love

Written in Vampires Blood: The Stranger

"Bound by Honor, Betrayed by Trust." -Foreigner

Table of contents

POLITRICKS: It's all political...I

COPYRIGHT © 2021...II

PLEASE CHECK OUT OTHER BOOKS:..III

TABLE OF CONTENTS IV

INTRODUCTION VI

WHAT'S YOUR DEFINITION OF A MAN?...8

MAN DEFINED...10

IN THE KNOW 14

I MUST CONFESS..16

A PARTY AIN'T A PARTY UNTIL WE VOTE YOU IN 17

IT'S NOT THAT EASY BEING WEED 21

IF LOVING YOU WAS WRONG 23

FORNICATION UNDER A CHRISTIAN KING.......................................25

PARADIGM..27

WHAT LIES BENEATH THE SURFACE? 30

POINT OF VIEW 32

FOUNDATION 33

A PERSON, PLACE, OR THING..36

I COULD REMEMBER BACK IN THE DAYS, SITTING ON THE PORCH EATING CEREAL 38

A CHANGE NEEDS TO COME! 41

TO BE… 44

THREE LITTLE GIRLS 48

A LESSON LEARNED 51

WHAT'S YOUR MOTIVATION? 53

PEACE 55

LIKE AND SHARE! 56

"BOUND BY HONOR, BETRAYED BY TRUST." –FOREIGNER 57

CRIMES AGAINST HUMANITY 59

A DREAM FULFILLED 63

BLOWING SMOKE 69

ARMS DISTANCE 71

PUBLIC SERVICE ANNOUNCEMENT 73

BENEATH THE OLD COTTON TREE 75

IS THIS DEMOCRACY? 80

REFERENCES 82

BONUS 85

A POET'S POEM TO POETRY (ODE TO SPOKEN WORD) 86

FATTY BOOM–BOOM 88

ONE PAIR 110

AUTHOR'S BIOGRAPHY 112

ABOUT THE AUTHOR 113

Introduction

Politics is a way to help the citizens when there are in need.

Except all the "*Politrickians*" can seem to do is feed.

Padding their egos and satisfying their insatiable greed.

Corralling citizens of the country like herds of cattle.

Eliciting aide from clergymen in a high power (In God We Trust).

But struggle to do the right thing when we're in our darkest hour.

As we stand naked, alone shivering, and vulnerable like petals that

were plucked off a delicate flower.

Do they love me, or do they love me not?

Dividing the country into two faction's nationalists and patriots.

Sacrificing the concept of democracy forever.

From the charismatic leader who delivers an inspiring speech.

But he/she is really a creep.

Having no regard for those who get trampled under feet.

Oh! the heart is willing, but the attempt is weak.

It is all the same if given the chance,

saying anything insatiable to save their seat.

Exploiting corporate ties and spewing white lies from their teeth.

Propaganda swirling around like worms from a bird's beak.

Chomping at the bit, chewing up public policy.

Projecting empty rhetoric

at the other side like live rounds at the enemy.

You can't let 'em stick 'round their liable to go for your throat.

Then kick you while you're down.

Changing public opinion about you
having them digging in your coat.

All sides are pulling in e'er which a way.
Telling us it is time to "Carpe Diem" (Seize the day).
Meanwhile not a thing is getting done.
A slow arduous process gift wrapped so nicely in red tape.

With wonderful surprises inside just baking in the sun.
Debating internal deals is measure of the sum.
Creating animosity others and resentment for some.
There are no wins here how the government is run.
Ask yourself who is truly benefiting?
When most feel "Poli-tricked" and handled like their dumb.
It's impossible to discern the real from the fake ones.
Because most of our leaders are irrational bums.

–Matthew Dale

What's your definition of a man?

Is it a smooth talker, a trickster with a slight of hand?
Suave, debonair, tall dark and hand-some like Clark
Gable or someone exotic looking like
Harry Belafonte or Sidney Poitier.

What's your definition of a man?
Does he possess a deep commanding voice tone
like Barry White, or James Earle Jones?
A hopeless romantic, extremely confident, with swag like Jerome.

What's your definition of a man?
Assuming that you've been courted since birth,
way before you were ready for the attention,
and understood your worth.
What was the best approach/line you've ever heard?
Did it come from an alpha- male, a fuck boy, or was it a nerd?

What's your definition of a man?
Is he one whose masculinity and sexuality is unambiguous?
What about a paramour that piques your interest?
What turns you on?
What excites you?
Is he a man that's not intimidated by a strong woman, values her
opinions, and embraces her intellect?
Does he need to have the same standards
and religious beliefs as you to garner your respect.

What's your definition of a man?

Is he the one who puts up a façade,

concealing his true intentions with deception?

Does your defined man profess his true feelings

by overtly proclaiming his love

for you, clings to your every word, moves,

and put you on a pedestal high above?

What makes you crazy in love?

A good stroke, or a good joke?

What is your ideal mate?

Is he tall dark and handsome,

or is he mysterious, unpredictable, and then some?

What is your turn offs?

Is sex more pleasurable with a stranger (a one-night stand)?

Or... with someone that will take the time to know your mind,

is okay with spending quality time

and would be quite content just holding your hand.

Man defined

Above all else, before considering a man,
putting God first, must be primary in his religious conviction.
For him to receive my hand, my undivided
attention and utmost devotion–he must be R.A.R.E
(Respectable, Accountable, Responsible, and Exceptional).
That acronym is key to engage with me
verbally, mentally, and physically–be an asset to me.

As I attempt to achieve a semblance of peace.
Be present with me in my happy place.
As we both inhale (breathe in),
exhale (breathe out), relax, relate, and release.

Before he becomes my King, or even begin
to stoke the embers that lies deep within.
He must take the time to understand what moods I'm in.
Holding me down
all the while wearing his crown.
Putting himself on the line, all the time for me.

He will encourage my desire,
possessing the power to set ablaze my internal fire.
Percolating my burning desire.
Soothing the aches between my thighs.
Staring passionately in each other's eyes.
Caressing, intently trusting,
but not neglecting all my erogenous zones until we tire.

A real man is strong enough inside, not necessarily physically buff

but, he's disciplined enough

to be gentle, a hopeless romantic, and does things off the cuff.

Self-assured (but not arrogant),

masculine, true to his word and calm.

The most important thing is that he loves and cares for his mom.

Let's me know that he will treat me like a Queen.

Makes me burst at the seams–

to the point where I must scream!

Beaming with jubilation

with his intellect, and mysteriousness is intriguing and exhilarating.

Adhering to the rules of engagement and the laws of attraction,

being but a mere parcel in the clutches of ecstasy.

Riding the waves of pure bliss, on to the shores of satisfaction.

I need a strong man who's capable of doing anything that he puts his

mind to, a great sense of humor but is strong willed.

Able to adapt like a chameleon to his surroundings,

with great communication skills.

He must be well groomed, manicured nails, and nice teeth.

Firm biceps and pecks,

strong working man's hands, and well dressed.

He must have a pleasant scent,

well put together as if he were heaven sent.

Some men though, refuse to acknowledge

a true goddess like Hathor.

As a matter of fact, he'll reject the calf let alone the cow.
A great man will understand and knows how to manage their past
traumas and what are their triggers.
He's sensitive to his privilege–
in a society that's built on a foundation of misogyny, but he figures;
that the sum of all fears is that the moral compass in a male driven
society would eventually conclude that the correlation between
women and the universe is relative.
And that notion is bigger than his pecker.

He must be tall not only in height and length,
but he must have a backbone.
Standing firm on his own two feet, proud and astute in his posture.
Level in his stance, the sole controller of all that he surveys like an
eagle perched on higher ground overlooking greener pastures.
A cornerstone in my life, head of the household (my rock of
Gibraltar). His position must be impervious to
flirtatious female's come-ons, lead-ons, and so on. Otherwise,
negative influences by their so-called boys.

Finally, he must be human.
He must see me for more than just a super woman, but a person.
Then we could build together as companions.

I respect the unity of how people fit together differently, from either
their ethnicity or religious beliefs, it seems to fit like a glove.

But I truly adore the seamless symmetry of black love

I also need to mention all who need not apply:

I Don't want no "short-short man,"

scrubs who can't ever measure up,

or down low brothers–who like to take it in the butt.

Alcoholics, criminals, liars, gangsters, losers, users, men with mental

instability (crazy, deranged) and physical abusers.

Mama's boys reluctant to leave the nest,

living at home with an Oedipus complex.

Dishonorable mention:

Married men seeking an entanglement.

I won't lie if I can't find Mr. Right–

I'll give Mr. Right now, a try.

Anyone else with unresolved issues in need of professional help

Please don't Holla at me playa! I won't Holla back!

No, no, no!

Because I could do better by my damn self.

In the know

Many have died, for their rights to learn.
Unconscious and incompetent, in areas where
deficiencies are concerned.
Once made aware that acquiring a skill
and its advantages, you'll yearn.
To be consciously competent and begin to hone.
Gaining confidence from practicing and
developing determination to earn.
Self-respect, distinguishing your ability to set the tone.
To live a life with a wife/husband and a home.
Then raise a child to have principles and morals once grown.

Education is the key to unlock
endless possibilities to make your own.
Miseducating from monarchies, dictators, and theories once shown.
What their truths was, and it has limited us all,
those doctrines should be burned.

It is extremely dangerous, in this dog-eat-dog zone.
Where the rules are stacked up against us, like a wall that\s firm.
Overstanding the trauma of our past hits home.
Knowing the fact that our four fathers were prone,
to physical violence, shackled and forced
to work their fingers to the bone.
Laboring and building civilizations weren't their first milestone.
Being direct descendants from royalty,

14

originators of alchemy, agriculture,
and mathematics, is the main keystone.
Breaking down the barriers, set by a caste system
enforced by the throne.
Thrown into bondage, in a system, with ideologies
that everyone has outgrown.

To emancipate oneself from mental slavery,
can't be motivation alone.
Doing research from Timbuktu to the New World,
once believed to be unknown.

Affirm information before claiming it is all known.
That's the only way to etch a place in the fabric of society, that has
already been sewn.

I Must confess

I have a confession to make.

The measure of success I may never face.

Because I don't brown nose, I never liked the taste.

I'd rather learn from my mistakes.

Then be beholden to someone along the way.

I'm afraid that I may never be blessed
in the progression of success.

My pride is my burden, I must confess.

This sin is my armor, protection from the rest.

I'm vulnerable to attack; I wear my heart on my sleeve.

My passion is my only weakness,

converting it into a strength I must achieve.

Fuel for the flame that burns eternal.

A constant reminder, I can't ever settle.

Forging alliances to achieve my ambitions.

Abandoning notions of doubt,

understanding that this is only the beginning.

A party ain't a party until we vote you in

Heads we win, tails you lose.
It doesn't matter what political party
wins the election–those are the rules.

"Those who vote decide less than those who count those votes!"
The most infamous politicians are the ones
who lead with a bark with more staunch supporters than bite.

The overwhelming feeling of needing to vote for a candidate purely
based on political affiliation in my opinion is irresponsible.

Those who have the right to vote should align with a politician who
has similar values and an agenda that represents change with a clear
vision looking forward in the direction of unity.

"99% of failure come from those who make excuses!"

Sowing seeds of discord in moments of discourse.
Given up nothing notable or substantial dodging all the actual
questions the public want to be answered, including the draft roll.
But during times of war, regular citizens could only dodge shrapnel.

"Those who are on the right side of history
set out to do the job right, rather than wasting time explaining
why they didn't do anything at all."
"We all need to find balance between action and reflection,
with all the distractions it can be easy to
forget that the world is a terrible place.
Especially without guidance and nobody

there in your corner to protect you.

So, we must stand up and protect ourselves."

"Education is the most powerful tool,

once it's used correctly, you can never lose.

You can only win or learn."

"Pride yourself in affirming knowledge gained for it will govern the

ignorant who mean to self-govern with no allegiances to pledge,

must first empower themselves with facts

that being informative gives."

"Almost everyone alive can withstand adversity

without quivering like a coward.

But a true test of character is after they're given power."

"In the times of indifference, with our unwavering ability to

persevere our system should never collapse."

"In the areas where people are affected from draught, from poverty

our system should never collapse."

Perhaps, if we worry less about action but raise an eyebrow to

inaction when there's a clear call for action.

"The world would improve through change, and if we change often,

we will thrive towards perfection."

"If we can't revel from failure to failure.

If we have control in the present, we had control in our past.

We will appreciate the breakthrough

when approaching success in our future."

"Capitalism can be filthy, it can be gross, repugnant and alienating.

It can cause war, hypocrisy and fruitless competition."

"Which only leads to revolution, which is not a bed of roses.
It is a brutal conflict between ways of the
past and the progressive solution of the future."

It's widely understood under a communist leader that the
government dictates what it's citizens can do.
But it is less known in a Democratic Republic that; it's all about
what you can do for the government.
"Ask not what your government can do for you!"

"If your actions inspire others who are dreamers on being more,
they'll aspire to learn more, to become more and do more as proud
citizens; then you are a leader."

"The only way to achieve longevity starts with a healthy governing
body. Affectively defending against being undermined threefold;
with patriotism, a moral compass, and a strong belief in spirituality."

"Leave no stone unturned, leave it all on the line today, leave no
room for sorrow, leave nothing on the table, leave no space for
chance to doubt tomorrow. Leave no limit for the promise of a
progressive future promoting the importance of everyone's culture."

Please understand that "Both wings are attached to the same bird,"
so just sit back, relax; watch it soar with your own two eyes.
Admire it in all its glory and plumage.

POLITRICKS:

Just think we the people were not solely responsible for launching it,

until the wind carries it higher and higher
balanced and hovering above you.

Just ask the electoral college,
A party is and will always be a party, even with or without you!

It's not that easy being weed

Having to content with the laws of the land
that dictates where, when how or who can use me.
I think about how much easier it would be
as an agave plant, sugar cane, poppy seed,
tobacco, hops, barley or even a cocoa plant.

It's not easy being weed.

It seems that rules are stacked up against whoever I appeal to.
Even though people seem to be much happier
having me around, passing me around
to their friends at parties.

I help those who have bad nerves, can't cope with pain they suffer
from, or don't have any appetite at all.

It's not easy being weed.

There're all the different types of weed like
hemp, indica, sativa, ruderalis.

Some hybrid types of Marijuana have different names like
white widow, purple haze, sour diesel, or afghanica.

The different varieties of cannabis can be turquoise like the ocean or
have hairs on the buds as white as the tops of mountains, colorful
and sticky like bubble gum or just plain green like trees.
Some strains are high in CBD while others are high in THC
like sinsemilla, or even higher with cannabinoids

21

that can cause people to have the munchies.

Be cool, calm, and forgetful as can be.

When I and other members in my family are legal everywhere, they
could plant my seeds freely without worrying,
and everyone would be so tranquil.
I don't know why the different strains aren't legal already.
It kind of make you wonder why, but why wonder?
Legalization is inevitable.

Be green with envy it's fine, roll up, toke up, eat weed raw like
salad, chew weed as gummies, inhale the smoke from rosin, and
even enjoy weed inside brownies.

Just feel ire!

It's all good!

After all,
I think it's what I want to be.

If loving you was wrong

I've been asked on numerous occasions
if it was love at first sight between me and my wife.
I always said no, what was more important was that we were still in
love after our first fight.

It's nice, to be courted, lulled away, then swept off your feet.
But to have longevity in any relationship, you must have balance,
don't get off-putt by times when the ends don't meet.
Find a happy medium, so you'll recognize when your significant
other is being sweet.

Don't lose yourself in someone else's ambitions,
that's how resentment sets in.
Refrain from stroking their egos because it's like adding fuel to a
blazing inferno. Or aligning yourself with the eye of the storm each
time it blows wind.

Try not to keep tabs on how often they are wrong, and you are right
(even if it's true).

Being supportive and paying each other with compliments is the
most valuable thing you could do. (You could take it to the bank).
Never engage in the dangerous high stakes game of who does more
for whom. (Where nobody wins).
If you do, you may be setting yourself up for failure and
disappointment begins.

It's simply about a warm hello, an edifying embrace.

Hating long goodbyes, a term of endearment
said in right tone, could bring a smile to their face.

The terrain is rough on the course ahead,
pay close attention to the signs.
Be adaptive like water and erode a path,
moving forward together forever through time.

Savor every moment like a delectable morsel, great with each bite.
So, if loving you was wrong! I don't want to be right.

Fornication Under a Christian King

Under the blanket of the stars, behind a dumpster, in the rear of a
convenience store; we enjoyed a quick f___k.
We didn't have a care in the world,
or who saw us, we didn't give a f___k.

"Pump harder, pump harder," she said.
"I would if you'd shut the f___k up," I said.

Was it exhilarating?! Yeah! I skeet, skeet,
skeeted and I think she got a nut.
If she didn't— f___k it! I'll take the blame, it was an intense
pressure situation, I won't past the buck.

"Sugar, Honey, Iced, Tea! The cops!"
"Focus and be cool fool, they aren't going to roll up,
all they want is f__ing doughnuts.
Or maybe a Slurpee," she said.

"If you are offering, I will take one too! That donkey is too *booty-
full*, and I came too soon," I said.

"Ooh! You nasty f___k you think I'm a cluck,
if you want me to big gulp, you better pass me a few more bucks."
One cop noticed the commotion of us f___king and stuff.
He approached and asked, "What are you two doing back there?
From here it looks like you two are f___king and your ass is bare!
I could see your ___ or her tits I'll arrest you both, and you will
spend the night in the clink," he asked.

"It's Nuttin; dummy," I replied.

"Excuse me!"

"I mean nothing honey!"

I tucked my d___k in my jeans, In between the seams,
trying to hide what it seems to be.
But I was harder than the rock of Gibraltar.
More erect than a man standing at the altar.

The cop said, "I've seen enough to put you both under arrest

For indecent exposure, I could see your d___k and her breasts."

I replied, "Officer, before you handcuff us could ask you one last
thing. Are we governed under a democracy or a monarchy?"

"Excuse me!"

"If we are truly living in a democratic society than our indecency
that you claim was occurring would not be considered
Fornication Under a Christian King."

"You have a point, but smoking marijuana on private property is
illegal, so I'm locking you up for that joint!" replied the cop.

"Now turn around and put your hands behind your back."

Paradigm

Follow me on a journey of Our story's past.
A polarized figure, of whom you ask.
A man of honor, direction, and purpose.
Someone during the period of the coronation of
Haile Selassie but *H.I.M* isn't the focus.
A Jamaican national by the name of Leonard James Howell or "The
Gong," Gong Guru Moragh. He was vocal about God's chosen
people and presented facts that rivaled the slave masters.
The first preacher of this movement
became known as, "The first Rasta."

His position was named after *His Imperial Majesty* who was the
idea, and the paradigm for the African diaspora.
The crowned king of kings, lord of lords,
and the conquering lion of the tribe of Judah.

Emperor Haile Selassie I of Ethiopia.

Gong Guru authored and published the book,
"The promised key," dismissing the lies about the
black race that started clearing up the mist.
By teaching the people our truth,
landed him in prison for being a seditionist.
Although he didn't adorn dreadful locks, his work not only pushed
black, but the Rastafarian movement also went against the
establishment, and against the status quo.

Risking life and liberty for the progressive improvement
for black people globally, just so you know.
In my opinion, he should be a national hero!
Alongside Maroon leaders, 3 fingered Jack and Captain Cudjoe.

Although his teachings were well-received
by the people, and very inspirational.
It was regarded as hate speech, propaganda, communist rhetoric
The spread of his teachings and Marcus Gravey's
Pan-Africanism was monumental.
Fearing further backlash, he established a village in
St. Catherine called "The Pinnacle."
Where free former slaves in Jamaica
became self-sufficient cultivating Ganja.

For the government to have probable cause,
the village was viewed as a commune, purporting to be a socialist.
So, the walls had to come tumbling down.
The government had police raid the settlement in the 1940s, 1950s to
suppress black peoples progress, and for being defiantly independent
of the rules set by the crown.
Parliament could not stand idly by while wealth was generating by
the hands of the black and brown.
So, a militia destroyed it and cleared out the settlers out of fear of the
vibration of truth about black power and sound.

But it was too late!

Just like the maroon towns in Trelawney, and

St. Thomas centuries before them.

Smaller settlements upholding

the same principles started popping up around.

the country where poor people were fed up,

and eager to chase those crazy bald heads wearing wigs, out of town.

What lies beneath the surface?

What lies beneath the surface is it deep?
What's above the glass ceiling? Can you reach?

The pied piper leaves behind a trail of tears
by alleviating one pestilence for the next.
In the wake of his departure is social unrest.

The feat of walking on water should not behold but beheld!
In our hearts and minds, focusing on the examples set by our creator
that's higher than our selves.

As tempers flare hot as ashes from embers
remaining level on your square is a must
Don't dismantle your core values
for what can be found on the surface.

(Have patience)

Just imagine that it takes millions of years
before the pressure that builds up in the center of the earth could
make precious stones from dust.

Many Men of the cloth don't really
represent the word and laws of God.

They facilitate a means to an end, upholding a façade
Anytime these clergymen get caught breaking the commandments,
they're just moved to a different Parrish, same moniker, same job.
It was once said that "I must plant my seed inside fertile soil."
He achieved that goal secretly behind closed doors.

Until a great man exposed the sewn seed to the world.

He was then considered an uninhibited
weed who could ruin the bran.
So dishonorably the flock was used to pacify him
for showing the germ by revealing the plan
In the land of the unjust, the just are vilified, and slandered to the
point of a momentary lapse of judgment
cause the pressure seeped through.

Then they'll be used as an example for others to view,
that they too can be broken in like a shoe.
The greatest fear of the wicked is the will of the meek,
for he was promised this domain
If you have eyes to see,
ears to hear and a voice to speak
but exclaim to take a vow of silence.
Everything will remain the same without any progress.

Point of view

Why are you so weary?
Cynical, quite contrary.
The type that sees the glass half empty and not half full.
A straight arrow takes no bull.

A conspiracy theorist, devil's advocate.
An esoteric knowledge connoisseur,
much like Diogenes–a kynikos.

The pressure of upholding the status quo is secular,
and not on your shoulders it's on mine (the world).
Pure like a newborn baby, an autistic person, a beautiful mind.
There's truth in honesty, it cuts through the rigmarole
and in its purist form, can be more caustic than lye.
Setting a foundation upon principal,
social standards to abide by.

Secrets has been revealed to you already,
as for the world, it will take time.

Foundation

This one is for the culture.
Rhythmic, melodic sound and vibration of nature.
Rapid movement of the feet, swaying of hips.
Repetitious chants to pay homage to the ancestors.

Deliberate loud pounding of the kettle drums in succession.
Evoking the spirits on sacred ground.
Traditional ceremonies, offerings to the Gods
in temples or around burial mounds.

Then our people were abruptly captured (by Colonizers),
who enslaved our four fathers, and mothers.
Then they were transported across deep waters
to the shores of stolen land.
Our ancestors were violated and integrated with the native
inhabitants who share the same origins as the original man.
They all had the same principles, faced the same plight and atrocities
of a stolen legacy–in comradery, they band.

Together they devised a plan–developing then implementing a
system (Guerrilla warfare, prayer, incantations)
and a different language called "Patwa."
It all came full circle, connected by their roots in the mother land.
Warriors like Nanny, Ancoma, and Quao posted forts in the
mountains, then soon after setting up marooned communities, fought
for their freedom for centuries against the oppressors.
After the war ceased, poverty increased,

then they were looked upon as the aggressors.

Their disgruntled souls, and combative spirit out of Africa passed

along their rebellious nature

of those original people to their successors–

their legacy lived on.

Through the voices out of many, one people's struggles were heard

from Jamaican abolitionists like Sam Sharpe, and Marcus Garvey

who advocated against what was wrong.

Recordings of our stories past along in forms

of modern-day rendition of oral traditions.

By the musicians and singers like

Desmond Dekker, John Holt, and Toots and May tails

in the form of ska, rock steady, and roots reggae.

A natural evolution that passed the proverbial baton.

To artists that were inspired by their musical influences and distant

past, started a new genre of music by the name of dancehall. A war

cry by artists like Dennis Brown, The Wailers, and Burning Spear.

Reported current events of the horrendous conditions in the garrisons

that people of the outside world needed to hear.

A motivational speech to ease the pain

of the low-class citizens by acts like father

U-Roy, Tony Rebel, Black Uhuru, Gregory Isaac

sang songs of warnings to beware.

An emergence of sound systems like

Stone Love, Kilimanjaro, King Jammy, king tubby comprised of

turntables, mixers, selectors, and Dee Jays like

Yellow Man, Eek-a-Mouse, Supa Cat who paved the way for

Bounty Killer, Buju Banton and Jr. Gong.

A unique blend of Poetry, Jazz, R&B,

Rock paired with heavy bass and treble.

Was fresh and very different from everything else

is what makes it special.

A raw, gritty, unapologetic movement, a shift in the paradigm,

vibration of heavy bass and treble, the anthem for the ghetto– could

be heard from miles around and beyond the island,

from top ends, tweeters, and speakers.

(Coming back full circle).

This one is for the culture.

Rhythmic, melodic sound and vibration of nature.

Rapid movement of the feet, swaying of hips.

Repetitious chants to pay homage to the ancestors. Take it from the

top, back to the start of where it all began.

So, Griots, researchers, scholars, selectors

"Pull Up! And come again!"

A Person, place, or thing

Crossing paths with a black cat is bad luck.
An outcast is a black swan, black sheep, or an ugly duck.

Black thought is bitter, glum absence of hope and worsens with time.
Formidable words describing black, above a black line.
Indoctrination with these negative connotations of the status of black
embeds deep inside the psyche of a black mind.

This hate stems from the fear of a black planet,
history have already seen.
It began with the Aboriginal (Gweagal, Ainu, Andamanese),
Etruscans/Minoans, Olmec Xi,
Dravidians, kingdom of Aksum, KMT,
Batwa (Bess), The Great Zimbabweans, and The Empire of Mali.

Jealousy reigned supreme with the advent of
"The Red Shirts, and "The White League."
Many were against the spread of "The Fusion Party," nationally.
People who opposed forward thinking and inclusion
castigated many, by implementing "The negro rule."
During the "Jim Crow" era scare tactics was used.

Lynching's, beatings, literacy tests, vagrancy laws,
poll taxes and burning whole city blocks to ash.
These were amongst the documented acts that were cruel.
In 1873 Colfax, LA dubbed, "Red River," In 1898 Wilmington, N.C.
In 1906 Atlanta, GA. In 1908 Illinois,
dubbed "Springfield Massacre."

1919 dubbed "Red Summer:" In Charleston, SC, In Omaha, Ne,

In Ellisville, AL, In Elaine, AR, In D.C, In Chicago, IL,

In Knoxville, TE, In 1923 Rosewood, FL. "Osage reign of terror,"

Osage, Ok 1921-1926. Not to mention in 1921 Greenwood, OK,

"Black Wall Street" too!

Empty rhetoric fueled by bigotry, gas light swarms of enraged mobs

like they intended to stage a coup.

Sworn to protect the chastity of white womanhood

from burly black brutes.

A black light is normally used to see

what can't be seen with natural light.

Fight or flight, the story behind the black races plight.

Black soles, marching in one accord for what's right.

A black fist is usually formed due to a forced hand.

Raise it high against oppression, as it exudes black power!

Reflecting the image of a proud black man.

I could remember back in the days,
sitting on the porch eating cereal

I could remember back in the days, sitting on the porch eating cereal.
Living in the only city where you could go to any bodega for a hero.

My father came close, but he wasn't harder than crack rock
from either redtop or blue tops, both of which were beyond reproach.

I am from the inner city, where they mastered redlining.
Not to be confused with silver lining.
Because being a product of the city that never sleeps,
being on cloud nine is hazardous for your health.
It's best not to sleep on no one.
Meaning, don't ever underestimate nobody.
If you get caught slipping, you'll be the one sleeping
(with the fishes that is).

The city was divided way before "Reaganomics."
The government gentrified Seneca Village to make way for
Central Park, they also laid waste to an otherwise diverse middle-
class neighborhood to make space for the Cross Bronx Expressway.
From crown heights to little Italy,
the city to the projects, uptown to the Hamptons.
You don't have to be an economist to see what's happening.
In between the cement blocks used as sidewalks, nothing grows here.
But there's erected buildings everywhere you turn.
From hopscotch to beatbox, stick ball to slap boxing with other
inner-city youth will certainly be rough.

Double Dutch to slugs, Scully to two hand touch there's eight
million things to do in the naked city that is entertaining enough.

Playing video games in the arcade to getting sprayed
with water from a fire hydrant.
House parties, hide and seek, red-light, green-light, one-two-three.
Doing the dozens, kicking it with your play cousin.
Seven-eleven or catch and kiss.
To playing spades or sporting a high-top fade.
That's just some of the stuff we did back in the day.

Not every inner-city youth were "Wilding."
Those who did beat you in the head,
literally or figuratively speaking.

They did so out of desperation to procure
what they didn't have to survive.
The trickle-down effect always seemed to dry up
before the ones in need could benefit from it.

Working their fingers to the bone to make ends meet.
And still not able to afford anything much.
Is a hard pill to swallow, especially on an empty stomach.
I was taught that there is
two ways out of an empire state of mind.
Adapt or conform. So, many hustled hard, sell anything two for five,
trade food stamps, hit a lick, or get a jux or something.
But without accountability you
will end up trapped in the prison pipeline.

Designed by those who swore to protect and serve
everyone in the constituency.
But are only there to protect the interests of the
investors of the privatized prison system.

Throughout the years, reliving experiences with my peers.
I took heed to words of wisdom from my elders who cared.

If you choose to smile, hold your head up high,
look the man directly in the eyes.

Enunciate your words change your vernacular, shuck, and jive for as
long as it takes to get a piece of the pie.
Don't hate the players change the game.
I'd rather stand up and fight for my rights and die on my feet
then to live on my knees.
I'm too proud to beg for things that wasn't meant for me.
Living by these codes of ethics is the only way to truly be free.

A change needs to come!

We all can't breathe without trees.
But "I can't breathe," when your knees, are on my neck, cutting off
air to my lungs and blood circulation to my brain.
It's a mystery that the ones responsible for upholding the law, would
create laws like, "stop and frisk," to legally be able to search for
someone to maim.
Riots and protests are percolating in the inner cities yet again.

Fighting against social injustice,
we need criminal justice reform right now.

The legislative body needs to enact a bill,
so the statute can become a law that states:
having a black or brown face doesn't constitute a crime face.

Us not being able to rise above suspicion
should not be the new norm.

Being black and disenfranchised in all nations is not easy.
We are "Mad as hell and are not going to take it anymore."

Saying, "Enough" is definitely not enough.

"The hunt is on, and we're the prey."

Government officials aren't on our side anyway.
Being powerless generations after generation
of constantly facing situations.
Where people violate our civil rights and or blatant disregard for our

lives and the lives of our loved ones, (sigh) our nerves are frayed.

Forming a militia and fighting
fire with fire isn't always the best way.

It is as if the only recourse without
consequences and repercussions is to pray.

Minorities are suffering from PTSD.

History will always repeat itself,
until the laws that govern the land is changed.

Victimized by social injustice:

Yeshua ben Yosef Hamashiach year 1

Nat Turner 1831

George Stinney 1944

Groveland 4 1949

Patrice Lumumba 1961

Medgar Evers 1963

Fred Hampton & Mark Clark 1969

Move Bombing 1985

Rodney King 1990

Malice Green 1992

Amadu Diallo 1999

Sean Bell 2006

Oscar Grant 2009

Travon Martin 2012

Eric Garner 2014

Michael Brown 2014

Laquan McDonald 2014

Tamir Rice 2014

Walter Scott 2015

Freddie Gray 2015

Terrence Crutcher 2016

Philando Castile 2016

Antwon Rose Jr. 2018

Botham Jean 2019

Ahmaud Arbury 2020

Breonna Taylor 2020

George Floyd 2020

Out of the root, doesn't bare strange fruit.
For those who witnessed it, "There, there."

To Be...

To be black, or not to be black?
That is the question! Moreno, or negro it's both the same.
Nigga, nigger or neither. In the Pecking order in our social hierarchy
the negative connotation denotes a human stain.

Is it better to be a Nubian or a Kemetic king? A moor, An Olmec Xi,
autochthon, or pre-Adamite.
Is this narrative the prophetic answer?
Or is it the same, just a little fancier.

We've been Christianed, we've been Moslemed, even Israelited–
missionaries, scribes, and friars alike, where commissioned and
appointed "Protectors of the Indians."

It was a reconnaissance mission!

Imperative to infiltrate our inner sanctum,
to teach us about salvation to gain our trust.

We were casualties of war!

Most of us were not taken from our native homeland then
transported to a new world, that myth should be a bust.
The Conquistadors, and Pirates became Colonizers, that changed our
language, subdued our culture, usurped Our-story. They stole our
birthrights then took our land directly from us.

I would be remiss not to mention that willful ignorance is bliss.
Like downplaying a "Peculiar institution"
how some southerners refer to what slavery was, and still is.

44

Relegating all factual events to migrant
African workers after immigration.

Such arrogance,

gross negligence,

disregard for checks and balances,

scores of misinformation instigated by the likes of Edward Pollard,

Jubal Early writers of the "The Lost Cause."

Dastardly efforts of the U.D.C (United, Daughters of the
Confederacy).

Incorporated a false narrative in textbooks such as "Prentice halls
classic: A history of the United States" published by Pearson.
This is the very definition of cognitive dissonance.

Whenever someone asked them to address the allegations honestly;
their initial response is allegedly, deflecting the question totally.
A knack of shifting the blame on others
and never accepting responsibility.

They never give an answer directly, beginning all statements with; a
counter question, or no comment, or I don't know
All in upholding the sanctity of the status quo.

What does it mean:
To be captured
To be slaughtered
To be led astray
To be downgraded

to 3/5ths a man allowed only to labor, breed and pray.

The 13th derailed the intent of the rebellion.
The Emancipation Proclamation was a stunt
politically that put the kibosh on our sovereignty.

A socioeconomic move by a capitalistic country ensuring that the
revolution for our civil liberties would continue till this day.
Only to be intimidated by confederate nonconformists,
afraid that their positions will be taken away.

The hands that picked cotton had to dig themselves
out from under all that bureaucracy.

Being free on paper was transparent.
They still had to endure being victimized
by a system constructed on a foundation of hypocrisy.

Shrouded under the wide net of Jim Crow, segregation, and vagrancy
laws. All because our skin resembled burned brass and hair like
lamb's wool. truly molded by the creator's hands out of clay.

Sauntering on with scars from lashes by crackers,
all the while overcoming the syndrome of Willie Lynch.
The black man has forged forward with hopes of freedom

in the spirit of the Haitian revolution,
Moorish science, Garveyite pride.
NOI, instilled value inside downtrodden men Centuries of turmoil
and conflict to be considered a human being again!

Ancestors help me remember

the King in me!

Ancestors help me understand

that our queens represent the earth, please open my mind!

Ancestors help me remember

that out of a "Womb-man" birthed the entire universe!

That fact has been forgotten through time.

Ancestors help me overcome

their agenda, for far too long we've all been blind!

Ancestors help me remember,

I surrender, open my mind's eye!

Ancestors help them remember–

there are neighbors in the hood too!

Ancestors help us,

we've suffered long enough, it's time!

Three little girls

Baby you're loved, and your mom and I adore you.

A gift from God.

The most important thing that we've ever done.

We vow to take care of you from this day on.

The sentiment of saying "I love you"

won't be the only thing we'll do for you.

Don't concern yourself about who, what, when or how.

Rest assured we have your best interests at heart,

since we could hold you now.

(Oct. 4, 2008)

When I woke up that morning and I looked over at my pregnant wife

slumber, while her belly resembled the rising sun.

Our first little girl was ready to come into the world.

Ten little fingers and ten little toes.

A blessing from the most-high above.

Pure as a soaring dove.

High lofty and sublime,

Aaliana this name describes you, but the path

you take will be what defines you.

Baby you're loved and we both adore you!

A gift from God!

You're the second most important thing that we've ever done.

We vow to take care of you from this day on.

48

The sentiment of saying "I love you"

won't be the only thing we'll do.

Don't concern yourself about who, what, when or how.

Rest assured we have your best interests at heart,

since we could hold you now.

(March 19, 2012)

When I woke up that morning and I looked over at my pregnant wife

slumber and seen that her belly resembled the rising sun.

Our second little girl was ready to come into the world.

Ten little fingers and ten little toes.

A blessing from the most-high above.

Pure and swift as a native sparrow.

Taino defines your name as a treeless plain.

Zavanaa, you're not defined by only your name.

Your namesake isn't the only thing that's original, like the

indigenous people from which you came.

Our two babies you're loved, and we adore you both.

Two gifts from God!

The two most important things that we've ever done.

We vow to take care of you both, from this day on.

The sentiment of saying "I love you"

won't be the only thing we'll do.

Don't concern yourselves about who, what, when or how.

Rest assured we have both of your best interests

at heart since we could hold both of you now.

(August 9, 2018)

When I woke up that morning and I looked over at my pregnant wife
slumber while her belly resembled the rising sun.
Our 3rd little girl was ready to come into the world.
Ten little fingers, and ten little toes.
A blessing from the most-high above.
Pure, shy, and majestic like a belted kingfisher.
As important and a necessity like the first drink of water
through a hallowed reed.

Naala, your name doesn't only define you.
Xayamarrie, you complete our family
and we're proud of your nativity.

Girls, you all are loved, and we both adore you three gifts from God.

The three most important things we've ever done.
We vow to take care you three little girls from this day on.
The sentiment of saying "I love you"
won't be the only thing we'll do.
So, don't concern yourselves about who, what, when or how.

Rest assured we have all three of your best interests at heart,
since we could finally hold each of you now.

A lesson learned

In life, you must creep before you crawl,
and crawl before you walk.
Walk before you run, and coo before you talk.

In life, you must listen before you learn,
learn before you teach.
Be nurtured before you're grown,
and traverse before you reach.

In life, there's seven tries, seven stalls.
But you must persevere through those failures
and stay positive through it all.
After staying the course
through those seven rises, and seven falls,
now you're prepared if chosen to answer the call.

In life, it's easy to live a lie when you lie to live.
It's harder to give it a try before you try to give.

In life, you can only reap what was sowed.
If correctly measured the benefits
are more valuable than gold.

The effects of this reverberates exponentially
like an explosion that's controlled (think of the Big Bang).
In life, the paradox of marginal utility
between the value of use and the value of exchange,
will remain the same.

Until the emphasis put on commodity and monetary gains,
would change, and won't outweigh the necessity
of natural resources needed for survival is sustained.

In life, it's insane whenever you continue
the same actions expecting a different result.
You almost will always be called crazy if you venture
off the beaten path without seeking someone to consult.

In life, humble yourself or be humbled by someone else.
We're all empty vessels seeking fulfillment from our higher self.

What's your motivation?

The ways of the world are consistently inconsistent.
There's no need to nurse it,
if there's no admittance–there's no patients.
The struggle for resolve is real,
high as the unmeasured cost of a free mason.
Televangelists and politicians make strange bedfellows,
led by avarice makes them increasingly persistent.
Our survival in the world of tomorrow is intrinsic on the global
cooperation of our world leaders who so far has betrayed our trust.
Now, to whom or what do we pledge our allegiance.
Cause we're prone to acts of violence
while our rights they're infringing.
Dawdling over their fervor of debauchery, fleeing from
righteousness, peace, love, or anything
progressive they're inherently resistant.
Raise your bible and use your firearms against insurgents from all
shit-hole countries with the blessing of God.
Blow the sons of bitches to kingdom
come but protect the synagogue.
The disconnect is astounding the two are socially inept.
It's unfathomable how anyone could re-elect.
The gap is wider than pride and prejudice,
from someone anorexic to a person who's obese.
A wealthy man to a destitute one,

a steady incline to a decent that is steep.

People with their eyes wide shut, are usually outspoken.
Wake up and look around with all three eyes open.

I'll bet if you take the time to evaluate the system,
you're not the one who's broken.

Don't get caught up in the bane of idolatry,
proudly perpetuating the bain existence of Cain.

The consequences detrimental to your mind, body, and soul.
The opposition are vengeful without mercy.
You won't be able to bargain with nothing less
than a pound of the flesh.
Resist temptation if you're able, or surely, you'll gest.
Consume to live off what God brought to the table.
Don't live to consume, you might corrupt the message to the womb.
The looming crisis severs the ties that bind the circle of life,
sentencing the children of our future to doom.
This curse stems from the sins of our fathers;
go ahead, call my bluff.
The condition of our world is not evidence enough.

The crest is salvation, constant elevation
towards nirvana, hovering above the mess.
Give glory to the Most High, that motivation is best.
Login to the akashic record,
connect kinetically to what is outward within.
Generating a toroidal energy, opening up is how it all begins.

Peace

The world as a whole is, in pieces.

As the violence and indifference increases.

The participants in this race, are left running in place,

while their pain from self-loathing releases.

The world as a whole is in pieces.

As the violence and indifference increases.

After the damages are assessed from the storm,

and the waters are all calm.

Who's going to take responsibility to right all wrongs?

The world as a whole is in pieces.

As the violence and indifference increases.

When there's no more room in the belly of the beast

because it's full from the feast,

only then, society can exact change, for peace.

Like and share!

Lights, camera, and action!
Audience applauds with standing ovation.
All like, and share.

Life, love, and satisfaction.
Public post on social media, and follower's reaction,
disapproves with emoji, dissatisfaction.

Like, and no share.

Time, effort, and money given without invitation.
Like a true fanatic, spends it all on a big budget advertised
production.

Like and share!

Give the same support to your friends,
or family member's dreams and aspirations.
Help them reach their desired destination.

So please...
Like and share!

"Bound by Honor, Betrayed by Trust." –Foreigner

Babylon is failing.
While my blood is put on fire during the overhauling
of my country of origin.
As this *"Shystem"* crumbles, I don't know, how or when,
I will be whole again.

My people were prematurely harvested from our land
and directly trekked across an ocean.
For the use of our hands, most of whom lay in shallow graves under
the ocean floor chained to each other like paper cut out origami.

Stretching from shores of home to the shores of the unknown.
From Sierra Leon to Saint-Domingue, with sweat dripping from our
brow and blood oozing from whelps on our backs.

We bare this perpetual burden like Sisyphus.

Knees deep in the trenches sustained only by bonbon te.
Protected by a shield gilded from pride.
Mixed with tears streaming out of our eyes,
covered by a cloak, conjured by the practice of vodoun.
Those enslavers tried to work us to the brink
of our humanity like the indigenous
people of *Hayti* before us, but our will wouldn't give out.
They devised a plan to conquer us with biological and psychological
warfare through racism, classism, and colorism.
But our immune system is stout.

POLITRICKS:

On August 22, 1791, led by Toussaint Louverture,
we started to revolt and fought our way
out from underneath subjugation.
Jean Jacque Dessalines aided in securing victory declaring
independence after the revolution, on January 1, 1804.

Trodden down the beaten path through perdition, yearning for
restitution, from the clutches of our captures,
with our stolen legacy in tote.

The Colonizers sealed the fate of some when they wrote,
their constitution on stolen land.

We survived the 1937 Parsley Massacre, propagated by Rafael
Trujillo from the onset of xenophobia.

We won't wait in vain for salvation.
Whenever, if ever, the rapture comes to fruition.

Crimes against humanity

Cognitive dissonance is a term used to describe PTSD of conquerors/colonists and or white supremacist. This state of mind develops after years of having to take on the arduous task of civilizing the uncivilized (I was being sarcastic). Anyone who believes that they're superior to another race because of their ethnicity; has a mental disability. Ironically, those who do, are religious and by virtue of this fact contradict themselves because this behavior goes against all religious doctrines.

The practice of systematic white supremacy are crimes against humanity. In every incident of systematic racism throughout history all over the globe, none of the participants were ever remorseful for their role in murdering millions of people (not to mention other unimaginable atrocities). An affect caused irreversible damages to indigenous cultures worldwide. All from their greed, blood lust, and ambitions of world domination.

Their only excuse for usurping cultures and purifying lands of indigenous people, were claims of "Devine Rights," and the fulfilment of prophecy. The convoluted idea that genocide was needed–was wrong. It was just an excuse to take control of natural resources from people that in their minds, were expendable.

They boasted that it coincided with the biblical narrative of the "Curse of Ham," or Darwin's "Theory of evolution." They used Biology and isolated studies to fuel the concept of "Eugenics,"

(From the Greeks) to purify the world from indigenous

cultures globally. It was ethnic cleansing pure and simple. A ploy to rid the so-called civilized world of the meek, to make way for the betterment of their purposed stronger breed of races. This notion is sick and in humane.

Those actions weren't needed for the progression of mankind. That process of purification whitewashed all other cultures accomplishments, so the power elite could take the credit of all the advancement of indigenous people throughout history.

The Assyrians, Babylonians, Mesopotamians, Egyptians, Persians, Mongolians, Macedonian empire, the Roman empire, the Ottoman empire, Nazis, Confederacy, and the South Afrikaans' government; are some of the civilizations that gained power through this system who fell under its own weight of absolution. Claiming to be a white supremacist is ignorant. Anyone who does–has an inferiority complex. Their intolerance towards any other ethnic groups has caused: Racism, Castism, Fascism, Marxism, Sexism, Imperialism, Colonialism, Apartheid, Willie Lynch syndrome, Capitalism, Xenophobia and is the catalyst behind domestic terrorism (terrorist groups like KKK, Neo Nazis, and religious cults).

The need for liberation is the result of this systematic oppression (Causality). The effect of which is how all civil rights movements spawned throughout history. Jesus spearheaded Christianity, European governments' bias toward the "Enlightened Ones," forced them to create secret societies (Illuminati). Protestants opposed how

Catholics used religion for monetary gains. Puritans decided to distance themselves from any so-called religious groups that weren't living righteously.

Haitians revolted against their oppressors. The American Civil War was a fight against slavery and all who wanted to continue that peculiar institution. East Indians fought against being exterminated by the British. Patrice Lumumba, fought against King Leopold and Belgium's deadly imperialistic rule over the Congo. South African's fought tirelessly against apartheid. Allies fought valiantly against the Axis of power in WWII and Hitler's claims of riding the world of non-whites, Jews, and gays; to start a pure Aryan race. Labor unions fought for equal pay in the workplace. The Pan African movement set out to instill African pride inside anybody who's apart of the diaspora.

Moorish science of America movement sought to enlighten African Americans of their roots and place in the world. Nation of Islam taught the black man that they are the lost tribe of Shabazz. The Rastafarian movement sought to announce that Haile Selassie I (King of kings, lord of lords, conquering lion of the tribe of Judah,) was the direct descendant of King Solomon. And H.I.M was proof that the black race was never meant to be enslaved. The Black Panther party taught African Americans about their right as American citizens.

The government in this country viewed blacks as three fifths a human and treated as second class citizens. Civil rights movement exposed the unjust laws in America, and they brought about change.

It's unfortunate, that historically in societies across the globe, people either idealize you for being extraordinary or vilify you then try to kill you for being different. The social standard is to misjudge people based on appearances and by unaffirmed ideologies. No one ever bothers to take the time to understand anything. It's too easy to fear what they can't understand and hate what they can't conquer.

Every individual should search within themselves to gain strength and connect with their higher power. Acceptance starts with self, and then continue through inspiration. Humility is societies only way toward atonement. Putting God above all would prevent anyone from looking down on anyone. When everybody understands that there is a higher power than one's own self, the journey towards tranquility would be a humbling experience for us all.

A Dream Fulfilled

The year 2021 marks a half-century since the
"I have a dream" speech.
Over the decades there has been setbacks and obstacles, for those
disenfranchised, downtrodden people eager to seek.
The threshold of the promise land. But against all odds, our society
has surpassed where no one thought we'd reach.

Through the centuries, great leaders of their times
stood up against oppression.
Going to bat for the civil liberties that we take for granted.
Our four fathers and mothers fought tirelessly for our progression.

The mere suggestion of freedom and equality in this complex social
construct; made them public enemy's number one.
The smouldering heat and ambers from the flames of injustice;
kindled a path through the tunnel for them to run.

But the shackles of discrimination reinforce
the unfair laws of the land.
Separating "The Man" from man. An elaborate plan, barring us from
reaping the fruits of this land nor
the opportunity at pursuit of contentment.
Even though the crops were cultivated with our bare hands.

Their only interest is to uphold the interest
on the money earned by elitist off slavery.

This is why we mean "By any means necessary."

This is why we "Say it loud, we're black and we're proud."

This is why we kneel, to heal the festering wounds given to us by a
system that has set a false precedence
that they're superior and we're not human.

Despite the resistance of the opposition, we've overcome.

From those instances of being asked,
"What are you doing 'round here?"
"License and registration?"
"Can I touch your hair?"
I bet any promissory note that Black and Brown
citizens of this nation wasn't included in the declaration
under the term "We the people."
We've been led by some pro-righteous teachers.
While some have been led astray by
crooked preachers motivated by the all-mighty dollar.
Living in the lap of luxury while most of us live paycheck to
paycheck barely able to afford to live in squalor.
But we're now using our power in numbers and influence.
To inspire the ignorant to become more
self-sufficient because it's evident
that our so-called leaders are negligent
and has turned a blind eye to the slaughtering of our innocence.
Paying for our cooperation with public assistance
and stimulus checks insulting our intelligence.

That we don't know nor understand what's really going on.

Betting on the notion that we would remain calm.

Even though we're being played like pawns.

Strong armed to go along with this ungodly union

between the keep all and the have none.

Slowly but surely, we're becoming privy

to the rules; giving us leverage.

Using the laws to our benefit after centuries

of them being used against us to our detriment.

This is the age of Aquarius, signs of the times.

We're building wealth and confidence.

Self-assurance showing integrity and ingenuity.

The notoriety yields respect and forges alliances.

Our communities have a wealth of knowledge.

Our strength is our reliance of ourselves;

with that only brings solace–

that the Most-high is pleased with our progress in the face of

adversity showcasing our prowess.

Our presence is felt now. We've been to the mountain top and
chiselled a path for the descendants of those who got whelps for
even thinking they were more than just the help. Or a notch on the
white man's belt. (Three fifths a human being). All praises due to the
most-high God, we've risen above the surface motivated with a
purpose. Our eyes are focused beyond the prize.

Opened to all the generational lies, surprises revealed to us
by all the brave men and women before us.

POLITRICKS:

The world is watching bracing themselves for an end game strategy
that may set us back to the seventeenth century.
But it won't work because the devil is in the details.
We've been hung up by our entrails.
Stuck in place like a boat without sails.
Encouraged to raise a family without males.
Told to pick ourselves up by our bootstraps
without laces and we still refuse to fail.

Forced to walk bare footed across fertile land.
Towards a place thought to be baron only to discover its soil is rich
with precious stones, vitamins, and minerals.
Blessings carried over from the covenant
between God and the original man.

The sins of the father have gone unforgiven.
We've walked through a burning inferno.

Shackled with chains and raped of our pride,
dignity, and sanctity of our abilities to change the channel.
So, we can showcase our true identities as the progenitors of a
kingdom that far precedes the Egyptian Pharaohs.

The revolution was televised for all who has eyes to see.
It was written down by scribes from oral traditions for those with
ears who heard but chose to forget and not believe.
We shall proceed, standing on the shoulders of giants.
Grazing on the fruits of our labours high above the clouds in the sky.
Standing eye to eye with the Gods of our distant past.

Traversing the pathways on a higher plane.

Trading history for our story,

studying the lines of the Akashic record.

Opening a dialog with the ether.

Not exchanging our souls for goals either.

Learning to Inform with know-ledge.

Embracing the journey to empower progress

not limited to a credo or pledge.

Free your mind first and the rest will follow.

Vibrating on a different wavelength,

creating a conduit to the ancestors telepathically.

Disciplined enough to achieve Christ consciousness.

It's obvious that ever since they discovered who we were.

The plan was predicated on spiritual warfare.

A race to devour us as a whole.

The key to the universe; has always been our soul.

Kicking us off the pedestal down to the low end of the totem pole.

Using our story against us as a form of control.

Behold, the pale white horse,

the fact we were attacked without provocation.

Yet they shown no remorse.

The devastation from their insurrection uplifts us to stay the course.

Inspiring one to reach one, so each one could teach one,

aspiring to be the only ones.

But there's still a lot of work to be done.

POLITRICKS:

Tearing down monuments and exposing
sundown towns isn't enough.
Holding people accountable for their actions
who'd otherwise be given a pass, is a must.
Working towards a better tomorrow hand in hand with the
lawmakers and the opposition; is the only way to gain our trust.

Breaking down the barriers that separate us
as human beings and not as a race.
Aligning with our moral compass
keeping in mind not to judge a man by his face or place in the
overall state of achievement in which our society is based.
We've marched until our skin chafed.
Protested immoral social injustices until we're blue in the face.
And still in this modern day, throughout the great fifty states, it's
still unsafe, to have a black or brown face.
For God's sake there's too much bloodshed
and not enough time to heal those wounds.
There're too many tears streaming down the cheeks of mothers while
stating "Daddy is going to do time, but he'll be home soon." The
path of least resistance is the road least visited.
With our arms clenched together as one people,
every religion, colour, or creed has been battle-tested.
Striving for the dream to be fulfilled.
So, our future is bright.
Things will be alright.
If we don't take a bite from a slice of the devil's pie.

Blowing smoke

We stand.

And on both sides, we fight against the left and the right.
We supposed to be bipartisan,
carrying on like children brimming with an inert hate.

Unable to reach over to the other side.
No empathy, no care, or sympathy for the constituency.
For the most part we remain quiet just along for the ride.

As they duck and hide the pertinent questions,
while mentioning the things they need not mention.
Now everything is in a force of contention.

Entangled with subjects that shouldn't be politized.
Yet somehow our resolve is tested and are begged to question.

How far will we go?
Sometimes I feel that it is all for show.
Promises are made, then swept under the rug,
with nothing more than a shrug.

Here's the case, the only time when politicians
hardly care about the base.
Is only when it comes time for them to win, (vote for me)!
magically blowing smoke in your face.

Where is the progress?

Money exchanges is always the basis.

POLITRICKS:

Let's tear it all down, so we can build back up,
but never do the latter.

Patronizing us asking questions like, "What the matter?"

Only when the vote is on the line, a seat is on their mind.
Rally their staunch supporters to come rally behind.

Using Politricks on us to believe in ideals like justice, patriotism,
civil liberties, foreign policy, and religious freedoms.
If you take a good look into yourselves—there is none.

Arms distance

Everything is at arm's reach, anyone who has internet access could order anything online, and it would be delivered promptly to your doorstep. Although adhering to social distance mandates worldwide, we seem closer than ever before in the history of humankind. With all the resources we have at hand, we share information, products, our talents, and our opinions all over social media.

With that said, we live in a fear-driven society, forced to fear known knowns and known unknowns. Many people have exhibited symptoms of social distance anxiety. Angst is at an all-time high. We wear masks and gloves for our protection and the protection of others day in and day out. But it cut off our circulation. It stifles our need for human contact.

Is this virus a natural occurrence? A reaction by nature, provoked by humankind's pollutants on land, sea, and air. Or is the pandemic caused by cross-contamination of bat guano and livestock to man?

Or is it a "Plandemic?" Forced upon us by elitists, trying to push their agenda and cashing in on vaccinations. As a result, all but guaranteeing population control.

This is not a black or white thing, nor is it a rich or poor thing, either. The coronavirus has taken over 500k lives nationally and 1.5 million and counting abroad. It has disrupted our lives, and for countless others, taken away our livelihood.

COVID-19 has affected us all. It is in everyone's communities and is continuously infecting our loved ones. Nobody is safe from this virus. Our mothers, our fathers, sisters, brothers, our aunts, uncles, and especially our grandparents are all susceptible to contracting this deadly disease.

For all those nurses, doctors, first responders, and military personnel whose job is to keep order during this otherwise chaotic time, let us band together to support the essential workers on the front line. They risk their health and well-being to make sure everyone else is safe.

We are all we have. We are in this together!

I want to thank grocers and those of us who are in transportation, who ensure that everyone gets what they need and get to where they need to go.

No one knows when this will end, but what's certain is that the year 2020 will go down in infamy.

Public service announcement

I work in a city where it is bad to be good, but it is good to be considered bad. I am a bus driver; some may say that my colleagues and me are essential workers. I do my part by helping steer people in our communities towards some sort of normalcy one turn at a time. But for others, I am the fall guy! A scapegoat, a human pin cushion. Here only to serve the public for them to project their issues upon us.

But I resolve confrontations mostly through conflict resolution, equipped with years of "Ambassador Training." With 15 years of service dealing with detours, service delays, blizzards and confronted with a constant reminder of customers reminding you that they are dissatisfied with service that day. I wouldn't have it any other way.

There's a reason why they call us operators, the system is like an artery. Each line keeps the people moving from point A to point B. Making every stop at each station, platform, or sidewalk is like the pulse of each town, ensuring that the heart of the city beats on.

This goes out for all the transit workers who lost their lives due to this covid-19 pandemic while on the job, let's have a moment of silence in remembrance of their sacrifice—R.I.P, and for those who tested positive get well soon, I salute you! My condolences to your valued loved ones who graciously shared you with the public. I should be angry and vindictive towards the public that I serve, but I am an optimist and I have a role to play.

I may not run a community service organization, but I do run an outreach program daily every time I adorn this uniform and board and alight passengers on my bus. Even with or without greetings or salutations, the irregularities the lock down and social distance caused, seems regular to me.

So, "Stand clear of the closing doors please!" I have a schedule to keep.

Beneath the old cotton tree

There's a story of a woman named Mary, whose child's grades declined in school. She tried everything she could to help him. She bought workbooks, set up study groups; she even hired a tutor. But despite their maximum effort, her son couldn't get over his slump.

There were murmurs around town that "Obeah" caused her child to become dunce. But Mary wouldn't believe that to be true.

Until dozens of parents in her district came forward to voice their concerns; one by one, they admitted that their children's grades declined in school too.

One morning, while walking her son to school. Mary noticed a crowd of people gathered on the side of the road around an old cotton tree. When they got closer, they pushed their way through dozens of people standing shoulder length apart.

In the crux of the crowd was a local farmer crouched in a hole by the base of the tree. His bare hands were wallowing in the dirt—fishing for what appeared to be a lunch pail. Drenched in sweat, the foul stench of anguish radiated from him as he dug deeper into the pit.

Every time he had a firm grip on the lunch pail, it suddenly sank deeper into the ground beneath the old cotton tree.

"Cum mon, mek we help him, nuh?" asked one man.

"No sah! Yuh si seh him is ah Obeah man! Cockroach nuh biznizz eena fowl fight," A woman replied.

"Cum on mon! Grab up di sumtin nuh," an elderly woman said.

Indiscriminate chatter drowned out the sound of the farmer's fingernails scraping against saddle stones and bits of coral. Angst grew amongst the locals as they stood around, astonished by the unbelievable sight. Two anxious men bent down and jumped into the hole in the ground beneath the old cotton tree. One of the men reached for the lunch pail and the farmer's eyes opened wide.

"Tap! Nuh touch it! Cum out! Nuhbadi else nuh cum dung inna dis sinkhole, ar wi all wud decent dung eena tuh di abyss widout ah certain return," The farmer yelled out.

Both men climbed out of the hole. The farmer wiped his face with a handkerchief, then continued with the task. He struggled for hours until he pulled the lunch pail from the clutches of the damned earth.

"Yuh bugga yuh! Mi git yuh!" said the farmer. Panting like a mongrel, he looked up and raised the lunch pail above his head.

"Mek haste an git him out ah di pit," The neighbours said.

Two men reached in and pulled the farmer out of the sinkhole with the lunch pail in tote.

The farmer dropped down to his knees and raised his arms in the air. In a trance, he screamed out some words that sounded like gibberish but was an incantation. Afterward, he forced open the lunch pail with his dirty and grimy bare hands. When the Obeah man pried open the pail, there were countless pencils, notebooks, hairbrushes, combs, and erasers inside. The parents of the students put their hands on their heads and yelled out, "Bumbaclot."

They shook their heads and asked, *"Ahuu wud ah target dem pickney yah? How cud sumady bi suh wicked?"*

They were all dumbfounded that someone could be so wrought with such malice and malcontent.

Everyone stood around the items of the lunch pail and held each other in solidarity. They prayed to Jesus for guidance during this otherwise bewildering circumstance.

"O Lord Almighty, thou God of Israel, hear now the prayers of the dead Israelites, and of their children, which have sinned before thee, and not hearkened unto the voice of thee their

God: for the which cause these plagues cleave unto us.

"Remember not the iniquities of our forefathers: but think upon thy power and thy name now at this time. "For thou art the Lord our God, and thee, O Lord, will we praise," [Baruch 3:4-6]

"Bac up! Mi gwine sen ih bac tuh whoever did dis," The farmer said.

Everybody took a few steps backward during his ritual. The farmer's voice grew louder, more baritone and echoed throughout the garrison. His head twirled around until the whites of his eyes were the only thing visible.

On the clear September morning, a dark cloud formed in the sky out of nowhere.

During the farmers' incantation, the clouds grew thicker and darker. Thunder rolled and electricity generated along the lining of the storm cloud. People panicked and ran away for cover. The dark cloud hovered over the old cotton tree.

Then, a single bolt of lightning clapped, struck the tree, and split it right down the middle. Blue flames erupted on the old cotton tree, then grew into a blazing inferno. After a few minutes, the flames disappeared, and the smoke cleared. A few people yelled out, *"Lawd Jesus of mercy! Cuh deh mon."*

A dozen more lunch pails emerged from the charred remains of the old cotton tree.

All the lunch pails spontaneously burst open one by one. Pencils, notebooks, pens, hairbrushes, and combs; spilled out of them.

From a distance, a loud blood-curdling shriek rang out from a run-down shack with a rusty zinc roof. The decrepit door swung open, and a feeble woman dropped down under the veranda outside the dilapidated house.

"Ah lie, Mrs. Brown cud'n bi suh wicked," One man said.

Dark blood oozed out of her eyes, ears, mouth, and nostrils like molasses.

The farmer collapsed at the same time.

"Lawd God him dead now," An elderly man yelled out.

"No mon, him cyaan dead suh, he a ah cunnuh munnuh; hard man fi dead," Another man replied.

People scrambled to catch water from a nearby well with buckets. They splashed water on the farmer. Somebody held the back of his head up as a little girl poured water into his mouth with her open palm. He swallowed some water, coughed, turned his head, and opened his eyes.

"Yuh aright?" asked the little girl.

The farmer shook his head, and people helped him up to his feet.

The crowd cheered and clapped for him as he took a few steps. He looked like a newborn fawn taking its first steps after birth.

From then on, people in the district urged their children never to lend anyone their pencils, pens, notebooks, hairbrushes, or combs. The stigma of Obeah grew, and the legend of this story spread throughout the Parish. Cautious parents of students from then on vowed that no one else would ever suffer from the same calamity. The misuse of "Obeah" stunted the growth of a few dozen students.

Some refer to it as "Juju." Others nicknamed it "Voodoo." There are different forms of "Vodun" originally from villages in West Africa.

It's said that the marooned people who fought tirelessly against slavery used it to protect themselves from the institution of servitude.

"Obeah" is shrouded in mysticism. Some people think it's just old Jamaican folklore. In contrast, others seek help from this form of magic to aid them in monetary advantages. Some people think that those who dabble in it to bind one person to another person; are bad-minded and evil.

Anyone who abuses this ancient practice won't succeed.

"Suh, lowe Obeah, an pray tuh di almighty fi guidance; Afta all, eh gud ova evil," Mi seh.

Is this Democracy?

We stand on both sides fighting against the left and the right.
Which side is supposed to be a bipartisan, or pensive?
Carrying on like children, brimming with a tense inert hate.

Incapable of reaching over to the aisle
unwavered of appearances,
of their peers through the fences.
Leaving us in a state of an extremist debate.
A twisted fate.
Numb to all the events; it's becoming increasingly
hard to separate, the real from the fake.

No empathy, no care, or sympathy for their constituency.
It's almost as if we are blindfolded on a
run-away succession, just along for the ride.

Oblivious to all the pertinent questions, evasive maneuvers
as they try to duck and hide.

Overlooking the obvious, only mentioning
things they need not mention.
The Truth for them seems to be a force of contention.
A farce smeared all over a political illustration.
Hmm–wonder why we can't heal the nation.

A wound cut so deep it will never be on the mend.
A ragged legion infected with racism, sexism,

bigotry, classism, and discrimination.

Dismissive of our intelligence, when the ones whom
we put all our confidence Just sweeps under the rug
every single one of their broken promises.

Only lobbyist is heard.
Purposing and signing into law the Bills
of Big Corporations mindless policies.

It's a never ending the cycle.
Spinning round and round,
case by case, time and time again.

Politrickians could care less about their base,
until it is time to win; then they're all up in your face.
Dammit, what we want is to be heard.
What we need is to feel safe.

Trillions in debt, prison reform,
defund the police, economic pitfalls.
Unemployment is too high,
minimum wage is too low;
don't get me started on gun laws.

None of them can't agree on healthcare;
why cause who the hell cares.

So, ask yourself, is this what we call democracy?

References

"A party ain't a party until we vote you in!"

"Those who cast the votes decide nothing. Those who count the votes decide everything."

–Josef Stalin

"99% of failures are the ones who make excuses."

–George Washington

"It takes less time to do a thing right, than it does to explain why you did it wrong."

– Henry Wadsworth Longfellow

"We all need to get the balance right between action and reflection. With so many distractions, it is easy to forget to pause and take stock." – Queen Elizabeth II

"The world is not the most pleasant place. Eventually, your parents leave you and nobody is going to go out of their way to protect you unconditionally. You need to learn to stand up for yourself and what you believe and sometimes, pardon my language, kick some ass."

– Queen Elizabeth II

"Education is the most powerful weapon which you can use to change the world." –Nelson Mandela.

"I never lose, I either win or learn." – Nelson Mandela.

"Knowledge will forever govern ignorance; and a people who mean to be their own governors must arm themselves with the power which knowledge gives." – James Madison.

"Nearly all men can stand adversity, but if you want to test a man's character, give him power." –Abraham Lincoln

"We have said we will never collapse, never ever. We may have our drought, our poverty, but as a people we shall never collapse, never ever." –Robert Mugabe

"To improve is to change; to be perfect is to change often."

–Winston Churchill

"Success consists of going from failure to failure without loss of enthusiasm." –Winston Churchill

"I find capitalism repugnant. It is filthy, it is gross, it is alienating… because it causes war, hypocrisy and competition." – Fidel Castro

"A revolution is not a bed of roses. A revolution is a struggle between the past and the future." – Fidel Castro

"Ask not what your country can do for you – ask what you can do for your country." –John F. Kennedy

"If your actions inspire others to dream more, learn more. Do more and become more, you are a leader." John Quincy Adams

"America is like a healthy body and its resistance is threefold: patriotism, its morality and it's spiritual life. If we can undermine these three areas, America will collapse from within."

– Joseph Stalin

"Whatever you do, do it with all your might. Work at it, early and late, in season and out of season, not leaving a stone unturned. And never deferring for a single hour that which can be done just as well now." –P.T. Barnum

"I call both the left and right wings socialism. And today, the right-wingers love to think that their capitalist, or free enterprisers, or what not. No, they're not! The correct name for this is left-wing socialism or right-wing socialism –and both wings are on the same bird." –Andrew Joseph Columbus

Bonus

THE PEN is MIGHTIER

THAN the SWORD

(A Chapbook)

By: James Dale

A poet's poem to poetry
(Ode to spoken word)

I learned that every line doesn't have to rhyme in a poem.
As long as the syntax is aligned, and my cadence is fine.
The poetry I recite will resonate when my words are spoken.

As the synapsis of my brain
Snap, Crackle, and Pop, with waves of euphoria.
And the syllables of each stanza
buzz in your eardrums like bees hovering over a petunia.

My message will reverberate when I demonstrate simile
in each verse like world renowned speeches throughout history.
Great speakers like Garvey, brother Malcom, Lincoln, or Kennedy.

I studied all the rules.
I didn't only rely on learning this in school.
I wrote and published works in anthologies and chapbooks.
I learned to love slam poetry after an open mic (school of hard
knocks): sinker, line, and hook.
I Gave it a Go–then I Got the Gist– Graphed it to my Glossary.
Gradually I Got Good and Girls/Guys peeped Game.
Groups Gathered that I had the Gift of Gab.
I Gauged, Gorged, and Grazed on each alliteration.
aligned in sequence like an incantation.
I retained each quatrain,
then recited it in repetition.

86

I adopted those principles to cultivate
another level of comprehension.
I unbound my mind and my imagination became form free,
lofty like the wind on the wings of a bird soaring above the sea.
I submitted to insight beyond sight to see.
I pay tribute to the art of poesy
by writing on the sands of time a letter that is open.
Now as a poet, I'm fine that every line doesn't rhyme in my poems.
Because my lyrics will resonate when the words are spoken.

Fatty boom–boom

I could remember it like it was yesterday. The very first time I heard the term, "Fatty boom, boom." It was circa 1986; my mother and I were standing outside of the airport in Kingston, Jamaica, waiting to be picked up by my uncle, Mr. Parnell. As we stood there hand in hand, I couldn't get my mind off how hot it was in Jamaica. The sun was high in the sky, situated just above the clouds, in all its glory.

The sun's rays roasted my ear lobes. My mother smeared Vaseline on them because the barber got too close with hot clippers and nicked them. My eardrums rang like an alarm clock from the plane ride. My mother clinched my hand tight when two men approached us. I looked up at her and said, "Who's "Norman Manley?"

My mother replied, "He was the Prime Minister of Jamaica. The government named this airport after him in his honor. Now, tap eeh nize."

The men looked at my mother and asked, "Taxi?"

One of the two men grabbed our luggage from the ground and the other man opened the trunk lid of his car.

My mother gasped and said, "No! see mi ride ah cum!"

Uncle Parnell beeped the horn, then he pulled up to the curb in front of us and yelled, "Santi! Wah gwan?"

He hopped out of the truck and whispered in my mother's ear, "Cum, mek hace before smaddy tek unnu weh."

Uncle Parnell was a tall and strapping man. He was dark-skinned, his hair was thin and curly. I heard my parents speak about him as they said he was "Cooley."

As he packed the luggage in the back of the pickup truck, I saw two faces glaring at me, looking over the side of the truck's side rails. Uncle Parnell said, "Unnu move an mek the bwoy come in wid unnu."

I climbed into the open back truck, and they both covered their mouths. Their shoulders motioned up and down, as they held back laughter.

"Him big eeh! Mi nah move, mek him go side ah yuh!" said the boy.

I kissed my teeth and squished my way in between the two of them on purpose after his snide remark.

The little girl kissed her teeth and said, "Hey fatty boom, boom, small up nuh! Mi nuh hab no space! Yuh wan mi go ova di side inna di gully?"

I stared at her and held my mouth open in shock by the insult. With my attention averted, the boy slapped me in the back of my head. The two kids laughed and slapped their knees.

"Look pan him a swell up lakka bullfrog. Yuh ah spring chicken?"

The two kids repeated the phrase over, and over while pointing at me and laughing! "Fatty boom, boom, fatty boom, boom!"

My face turned red as a radish as they continued to ridicule me.

I rubbed the back of my head, and tears welled up in my eyes. I panted, gritted my teeth, and grumbled.

I couldn't take it anymore, so I erupted and screamed, "Tap it! Nuh badda mi! Lowe mi before mi tump the two ah unnu!"

Their silence was deafening, until my Michael Jackson Casio wristwatch alarm, sounded off. They were both mesmerized by it.

The little boys' eyes lit up as he said, "Mek mi see it nuh, dat deh watch deh nice eeh!"

I thought to myself, 'I should be just as mean to them as they were to me and deny the request.' But I didn't, I just took my favorite watch in the whole wide world off my wrist and handed it to him.

They both ignored me the entire ride to our destination in Portmore. They were just too preoccupied with the watch. Every 30 minutes that passed the alarm sounded off and the melody of the song, "Beat it," by Michael Jackson would play. Three silhouettes of him doing the moonwalk displayed in succession across the screen of the Casio watch.

Uncle Parnell approached Aunty Mavis' house while the sun's rays shunned down from the heavens. Her house resembled a great white castle. The stucco glistened, reflecting the sunshine like a mirror or like how light reflects off the surface of a large body of water. We could see her standing outside the front of the house feeding chickens.

Although it was a rural setting, Aunt Mavis still raised

chickens. I guess the saying is true, "You can take the girl out of the country, but you can't take the country out of the girl."

Uncle Parnell put the truck in park, and Aunt Mavis said, "Santi! come, come give me a hug, mon."

My mother jumped out the passenger side of the truck and said, "Cutie, my long fi is yuh."

I, on the other hand, was reluctant to do the same. I was still teaming with anger from those two dry-headed, barefooted pickneys that teased me earlier about my size.

Aunty Mavis noticed and said, "Come yah bwoy! come give your aunty a hug. Wah happen, you nuh long fi si mi?"

I exited the trucks bed and sauntered towards her and said, "No aunty, dem did a bodda mi, dem call mi fatty boom, boom."

Aunt Mavis scoffed, fanned them off and said, "Mek dem gwan chat! nuh pay dem no mind hear! Dem a yuh cousins Chris an Stephanie, dem jealous dat ah foreign yuh cum from."

At that moment the two kids approached us with my watch in their possession and said in unison, "Ah dat yuh hab ah hot up yuh head Fatty boom, boom? Yuh don't have a worry inna di world, fi you bread buttah pan two sides."

Aunt Mavis said, "So Santi, ah wah you a feed di bwoy? Him too round mon!"

"Lowe di bwoy, him soon stretch out," my mother replied.

My aunt leaned over to me and said, "Aright mi nephew, what yuh wan mi tuh cook fi dinna?"

"Chicken!" I replied.

Aunty Mavis walked over to the chickens that were grazing, and grabbed one of them by the wings, held it up and wrung its neck. Then she tied its feet upside down off a tree limb. The lifeless chicken swung back and forth. The wings were extended over its broken neck.

Aunty Mavis grabbed an empty pot and placed it under the chicken. She grabbed a knife from out of the pot and slit the chicken's throat. The blood gushed out from its neck like water from an opened faucet. It drained downward over its beak profusely into the pot.

I witnessed this calamity at such an impressionable age, that I was momentarily paralyzed. It traumatized me so much so, I still have nightmares. I heard sounds and saw things I would have otherwise ignored completely.

I saw a large white cow with a bell around its neck walking up the street. I also saw a dark brown and red rooster strutting proudly around the yard as though it was herding the other chickens (hens) like a shepherd.

I couldn't stop staring at the jockeys' riding horses across the street in the arena around the racetrack. Propped up on the saddle, wielding an equestrian crop whip. They were in control of those majestic beasts. The galloping hooves of those majestic creatures made a sound when they trampled on the dirt, that was louder than thunder or one million drums being pounded all at once.

A crowd of people inside the arena and in the bar on the top floor of my Aunt and Uncle's house, were all cheering them on.

They all held small pieces of paper in each of their hands. I heard one yell, "Gwan sweet foot!"

I noticed the sign, and it read Caymanas Park.

At that moment, Uncle Parnell to my mom and said, "Santi mek hace an cum before di embassy too busy and yuh nuh get tru wid yuh son's papers."

"Ok! Mi soon cum, Mr. Parnell! Mek mi run go ah bathroom an cum," my mom replied.

Uncle Parnell turned to me and said, "Bwoy yuh a jus tan up deh suh all day ar yuh a cum wid we, eeh?"

"Nuh badda lef mi–mi ah cum wid unnu, Uncle Parnell," I replied.

After my mom used the restroom, she walked out of the house and got into the passenger side of the pickup truck. I climbed into the back of the truck. Uncle Parnell got into the drivers' side and started it. He toggled the shift stick, put the truck in gear and drove off.

The breeze blew on my face while I sat in the back of the pickup truck alone. I closed my eyes and took a deep breath of the so fresh and so clean, island air. The motion of the truck rolling over the rough terrain and the cranking sounds of the standard transmission, was peaceful.

I had a Zen moment, caught up in the fabric of time. I retained a semblance of peace, especially since those juveniles were not there to ruin my experience in Jamaica.

I opened my eyes, and kids much like myself, happily played

in the streets. Some played football barefooted. Some shot marbles, while others played with old milk cartons that they cut into miniature sized trucks. A bunch of other kids took turns using sticks to roll an empty car tire down the road.

On the sides of the road, there were who my parents' called hawkers or idlers (illegal street vendors) selling goods. They sold everything from clothes, cooked food, shoes, fresh tropical fruits, and artwork. This one-man steered a hand cart down the street yelling, "Peanuts! Bag juice! Wrigley's! Shrimp!"

I couldn't make out what else he advertised because we
moved too fast through the busy streets. It was teaming with the everyday life of people making something out of a bad situation, poverty.

I eves dropped in on Uncle Parnell and my mom talking about the reason for our visit to Jamaica. How she was there to file for my dad's older son Valin and that they needed to pick him up from Chisholm Ave. in Kingston. Then go to the embassy to get his visa and passport.

Afterward, all three of us would return to the states together. While I listened in on their conversation, it dawned on me that Uncle Parnell operated the steering wheel from the truck's passenger side. He also drove down the wrong side of the road. I turned my head around, and everyone else was too.

Uncle Parnell made a sharp right turn down, then downshifted the truck to slow it down. He raised his right hand
into the air to acknowledge a man he passed by.

I saw a single Billy goat with a bell around its neck trodden across the road quickly to avoid being hit by oncoming traffic.

A group of children younger than I was, walked down the street wearing school uniforms. The boys had on khaki pants with white shirts, and the girls wore blue dresses with white blouses. They were all making their way to school together.

We finally arrived at a house where dominoes clamored together as they were being shuffled.

One man said, "Wah mek yuh neva play tre s–eeh?

Yuh kno seh mi a run fram five di wul game. Yuh played tre five an, an mek di mon win back wit di big dutty double five. Yuh nah read di game mon."

Uncle Parnell beeped the horn to get the attention of the men. When they turned around to see who beeped the horn. One man said, "Ah who dat?"

Uncle Parnel said, "Ah mi mon! Valin di deh?"

"Yeh man! Ah mi mon," Valin replied.

My mother got out of the truck and said, "Valin, ah yuh madda, mek hace and cum before we miss di appointment."

"Ok, mi ah cum now!" Valin replied.

My brother stood up and towered over the domino table. He clinched his right hand into a fist and used it to touch the fists of the other three men still seated at the table. He said, "Mi soon cum."

"Cool nuh," one man replied.

The other men said, "Likkle more."

My brother Valin stood around six feet tall, and very lanky.

Jamaicans would describe him as Maaga. He was very dark-skinned and his eyes light up like a Christmas tree, as if he were excited to see us.

Valin walked away from the makeshift domino table towards a house that was near it. He yelled, "Aunty Ruby, mi gone! Mi madda jus cum fi mi, yah!"

At that moment, a short, older, and fair skinned woman stepped outside the house. She wore a floral one-piece dress, and her head was wrapped up by a head tie (handkerchief) with a floral pattern. She came out of the house carrying a small suitcase. "Aright mi nephew!" she replied. "Yuh gone? Tek care of yourself, hear! Nuh badda mek no chubble a foreign."

She handed Valin the small suitcase, hugged then kissed him on the cheek for what seemed like an eternity.

Aunty Ruby looked in my mother's direction and said, "Mawnin, Jennifer!"

"Mawnin, Mrs. Ruby!" my mother replied.

"Mawnin, sah!"

Uncle Parnell said, "Gud mawnin!"

"Unnu tek care of mi bwoy, hear! How's mi big nephew Calvin? Why him neva cum dung?"

"He cud nuh git di time off fram wok," my mother replied. "A jus mi an mi lass son cum dung."

"Weh him deh?" Aunt Ruby asked.

"See him ova deh suh, inna di chuck bac."

"Jesam peas, wata bwoy fava him pupa suh mon! Dead

96

stomp ah Calvin," Aunty Ruby retorts.

My mother nudged me and said," Gwan, guh gi yuh aunty Ruby a hug."

I climbed out of the truck bed and walked over to Aunty Ruby and raised my hands up to hug her. Aunty Ruby grabbed me up and kissed me like she was a bear grabbing for salmon swimming upstream.

"Wat a bwoy round and nice looking! Him fava mi sistah Mrs. Olivia bad."

After the onslaught of kisses, Aunty Ruby looked at me and asked, "Hab yuh met yuh grandma Mrs. Olivia yet?"

I shrugged my shoulders.

Aunty Ruby said, "It's aright, yuh soon si har an yuh grandfather, Moss Roy tuh."

After our greetings and salutations, Uncle Parnell, my mother, my brother Valin and I, still had to make the appointment at the embassy, which was a short distance away.

We all piled into the truck. As we drove down Chisholm Ave, I waved goodbye to Aunty Ruby

While the truck moved down the main road, my brother and I started talking to get more acquainted with one another. "Yuh aright–mi big likkle bredda?" Valin asked.

"Yeh man, mi gud!" I replied.

"Duh yuh lakka Jamaica?"

"Not really, mi cousins dem teased my. Dem call mi Fatty boom–boom!"

He burst out in an uproarious laughter, so loud that it caught the attention of my mother and Uncle Parnell as well as pedestrians on the street.

"Big likkle bredda, nuh watch nuh face, hear!" Valin said. "Dem jus jealous dat yuh cum fram forin."

The fact that I was foreign born, seemed to be a gift and a curse. "Why am I being singled out for being different?" I pondered to myself, while the truck slowly approached our destination.

Valin and my mother got out of the truck and walked towards the entrance to the embassy. My mother looked back at me and said, "Jamie! Mi soon cum bac. Be a gud bwoy while I'm gone. Your Uncle Parnell ah go deh yah wid yuh."

Uncle Parnell hopped out of the truck and searched his top shirt pocket for a pack of cigarettes. He took one out, put it in his mouth, struck a match from the box of matches, and inhaled the smoke from the lit cigarette.

"Yuh aright?" Uncle Parnell asked.

"Yeh man, mi gud," I replied.

"Yuh waan a bag juice?"

I shrugged my shoulders, and uncle Parnell reached inside his front shirt pocket and took out some coins and said, "Eeh, tek dis, go ah dat man deh an aks him fi a bag juice fi yuh, an a shrimp fi mi. Gwan! mek hace, an cum bac."

I took the change and walked towards the vendor behind the boxcar. As I reached close to him, I said with confidence, "Gud morning sah! Please may I have a bag juice and a shrimp."

The vendor smiled and replied, "Gud morning youth man!"

He extended his palm as I reached out my hand with the coins. He counted the coins in his palm, then handed me a bag juice, some shrimps and one single coin.

I took it and jogged back to where Uncle Parnell stood. He waited eagerly for me to return with his shrimp. I handed him the shrimps the change and said, "Thank you Uncle Parnell for the bag juice."

He shook his head and said, "Yeh man! Nuh problem!"

Uncle Parnell and I stood there and waited for my mother and Valin's return. It seemed like an eternity, but to a five-year-old boy, a ten-minute wait, felt like a lifetime.

Before long they both walked out of the embassy shoulder to shoulder carrying more documents than they both entered with.

When they got closer to where we were, my Uncle bellowed, "Unnu git tru?"

"Yeh man, everything crisp!" my mother replied.

My brother hugged me and said, "Cum, mi big likkle bredda, mek we cut out fram yah duh. Mi forin bound!"

We all piled back into the truck and Uncle Parnell drove us all back to Portmore, St. Catherine. Where he and my Aunt Mavis lived.

I thought to myself, "I hope she finished cooking dinner because I am starving. Then another thought entered my head, "But if she is–will it be that poor chicken that she slaughtered earlier? I'm not sure if I want to eat that."

Before long, we made it back to the house where Aunt Mavis was in the kitchen preparing a salad to complement the dinner that was simmering on the stove top. She baited her with time until our return from town.

We entered the house my Aunt's face lit up and said, "Mi glad yuh cum cause…"

I couldn't make out the rest because she dragged him by his hand into their bedroom and shut the door behind them. Aunt Mavis discussed with Uncle Parnell an occurrence that he seemed to be discontented with the precociousness of the story. Because he raised his voice tone as he reacted to the news that Aunt Mavis told him behind the closed bedroom door.

My mother pulled me along with her into the bathroom where she cleaned me up for dinner. After we exited the bathroom, she took Valin's suitcase and ushered him towards the room where he would stay for the night.

The two kids sat at the table and waited patiently for dinner to be served.

All the place mats were set, there were sets of knives and forks at each setting placed on top of a napkin that was neatly folded in the shape of a triangle. There were empty glasses turned upside down next to plates that were turned over as well.

My Aunt and Uncle exited their bedroom and he walked over to the head of the table and sat down.

Aunt Mavis walked into the kitchen where my mother was. They shared the dinner into dishes before they walked in the dining room and put it down on the table.

The entire house smelled great! My mother placed the first container on the table on a placement mat specifically intended for rice and

peas that she was carrying. The second container she placed on the table on a different placement mat, was the salad that Aunt Mavis prepared before we walked in the house.

My mother quietly finished preparing it whilst she discussed personal matters with Uncle Parnell in their bedroom.

My mother stepped to the side and Aunt Mavis placed down the chicken that she slaughtered earlier on a different placement mat. It didn't gross me out as much as I'd thought it would. The chicken looked so edible stewed in its own juices along with fresh vegetables that Aunt Mavis picked herself from the garden in her backyard.

My mother topped off the smorgasbord with a pitcher of freshly made carrot juice. I knew instantly what it was because my mother made it every Sunday for dinner. She knew it was my favorite thing to have, so she hummed while she placed it right in front of me at the table and kissed me on my forehead.

Valin walked out of the bathroom just in time, after the table was set.

My mother said, "Valin, cum sit dung yah suh next to yuh bredda.

Everyone sat at the table and Aunty Mavis clasped her hands together. "Bow your heads mem my bless di food," she said. "Heavenly father I pray to yuh thanking yuh fi di blessings in our lives and your constant presence during our stay here on earth.

Heavenly father please bless di food that has been prepared for sustenance in our bodies while yuh grace feeds our souls."

Everyone said, "Amen!"

There was minimal conversation going on at the dinner table. I of course was famished from the plane ride to the truck ride throughout two parishes during the long hot day. I surmise that everyone else adhered to the no talking rule while eating at the dinner table because nobody said a word.

After everyone finished their dinner, Valin volunteered to clear the table. He and Uncle Parnell headed towards the stairs outside the kitchen that led to the bar upstairs.

Aunt Mavis passed the two of heading outside while she brought the dessert to the table.

It was Pone, (sweet potato pudding.) It tasted better than my mother's recipe, I assume due to the climate and the fresh tropical ingredients Aunt Mavis had at her disposal.

I usually waited at least an hour after eating before going to bed. But I was dog dead tired, and we had to wake up early enough to make it to our flight, back to the states.

So, I asked to be excused from the table and went into the room that my mother and I were going to stay in for the night. I located my luggage and searched for my toothbrush and went into the bathroom that was adjacent to the bedroom, brushed my teeth and washed my face.

While I was gargling with water to rinse out my mouth. I

noticed that there was a lizard walking across the ceiling of the bathroom. I was startled at first but remembered hearing stories about croaking lizards from my mother and older brother Devon, put me at ease.

But finally, seeing one in person sort of intrigued me. It was green like blades of grass, and they kind of resembled branches, but with suction cups for hands and feet.

After I spit out the water inside my mouth into the face basin. I walked back into the bedroom and climbed into the bed. It was covered from floor to ceiling with a shear white cloth and

surrounding the perimeter of the entire bed. It was put there to protect my mother and I from mosquito bites while we slept or possibly lizards.

I noticed no other beds in the house was set up this way, I guess the mosquitoes love forin blood.

It didn't take long until I fell asleep. I remembered I overheard a conversation between my mother and Aunt Mavis. They discussed Uncle Parnell's daughter Claudette, who had got her visa a few years back. She filed for her son Chris and that the papers came through for him to go and live in forin with her.

I guess that was what the private conversation was about between Aunt Mavis and Uncle Parnell, when we first got back from town earlier.

I couldn't stay up long enough to eves drop any longer. My eye lids were too heavy; I fell out like a light.

Before long it was morning, I was startled out my sleep by

the roosters loud insistent crowing, "Cock-a-doodle-doo."

My mother was already awake, packing up the clothes in our suitcases, preparing for the plane ride home.

"Good morning sweetie," my mom said, then leaned closer to me and kissed me on my forehead. "Did you sleep well last night?"

I nodded yes in acknowledgement of the question she had asked me while I attempted to rub the sleep from my eyes.

"Gud, now git up an guh tuh di bathroom an brush yuh teet an wash yuh face. We hab tuh cut out soon to ketch di flight."

My Aunt cracked the eggs on the side of the frying pan, and they gurgled and sizzled as it hit the hot oil in the frying pan over the open fire on the stove.

I also could never forget the sound and smell of fresh cocoa beans, nutmeg and cinnamon as Aunt Mavis grated them into the pot of boiling water. Aunt Mavis scraped fresh vanilla beans in the pot, then sweetened the hot cocoa with condensed milk to taste. Then she stirred it all together back and forth with a spoon.

After a few strokes, she took a small amount of the enriched liquid in the spoon that she was using and put it inside the middle of her hand. Then she tasted it to make sure it was just right.

I could imagine her doing all of that whilst I was still in the bathroom because that is what my mother does back home most mornings.

After I finished up in the bathroom, I put on my clothes and left the bedroom. I sat at the table were place mats were set up for everyone that stayed at the house.

As I slowly sipped the freshly made hot cocoa my mom poured for me into a teacup, I heard a loud knock on the grille at the front of the house.

A voice said, "Cutie, Santi! Unnu deh yah?"

My mother got up from the table and went to the entryway and called out, "Jem? Gud mawnin, mi sistah! A wah tek unnu so long fi cum ova, ehh? Yuh nuh know seh mi soon cut fram yah suh?"

, "Mi know man, that's why mi come so early," Aunt Jem replied. "Yuh nuh know seh mi cudnuh mek yuh cum fram forin an nuh see yuh an mi nephew. By di way, weh him deh?"

Aunt Jem entered the house, she took off her shoes and said, "Gud mawnin everyone!

Glory be to God. How is everyone this mawnin?"

Everyone else seated at the table said, "Mawnin Aunty."

Aunt Jem walked over to where I was still seated at the table and said, "Cum yah mi nephew cum gib yuh aunty a hug an kiss."

I put down my hot cocoa and hugged her. At that moment two young girls walked inside the house carrying bags in both of their hands.

My mother hugged and kissed each girl individually and said, "Gud mawnin, Diane. Gud mawnin, Nikki."

"Mawnin, Aunty Jennifer," the girls said in unson.

Aunt Jem pointed at my mother and said, "Look inna di bag dem mi bring ova! Mi kyarri ova roast breadfruit, fried fish (scrat and parrot), gizzarda, drops, some tyme an ackee fi kyarri up."

"Thank you, hear mi sistah!" my mother replied.

I sat back down at the table and continued to sip my hot cocoa in it.

My mother walked over to the table and shared the breakfast Aunt Mavis prepared for us on the plate in front of me. It was fried eggs, baked beans, plantains, and toast. Everyone else was bust eating their breakfast, including my brother Valin, and Uncle Parnell. Who unlike everyone else seated at the table, they both drank coffee and not hot cocoa.

I didn't like the smell of fresh coffee; it always burned my nose. Coffee had too strong of a scent for me to handle, especially Jamaican blue mountain coffee. At least for me that is, it is stronger than Folgers that my father drank back home in the states.

There weren't any more space at the table for aunt Jem and my cousins Diane and Nikki to sit. So, they ate breakfast in the kitchen. They just took two slices of bread, a fried egg, and topped off with a dollop of baked beans and made sandwiches.

As they were stood in the kitchen eating their breakfast and sipping hot cocoa. I felt bad and offered my seat to Aunt Jem to take my place at the table. I finished eating my breakfast and wanted her to take my seat.

Aunt Jem declined my offer and continued to enjoy her breakfast in the kitchen.

After everyone finished their breakfast, my mother, Valin and I packed up our luggage into the open back truck.

Uncle Parnell said, "If unnu tek lang, yuh nah go mek di

flight. So, unnu mek hace an cum on nuh."

My mother and her sisters said their goodbyes. We packed up into the truck and headed to the airport without any further delay. I didn't realize if the ride to the airport was long or not because I slept the entire way there.

Valin nudged me to wake up as we arrived at Norman Manley Airport, in Kingston, Jamaica.

Uncle Parnell helped us with our language, and we all hugged each other, and my mother said, "Mr. Parnell, give thanks! We will si yuh soon."

"Aright Santi!" Uncle Parnell replied. "Lickkle more hear."

We walked inside with our luggage, and joined the line to check-in. The customs agent pulled my brother Valin to the side and asked him a series of questions that only he could answer. The interrogation didn't last very long, the agent stamped his passport and let him through.

We all sighed in relief. I thought about the sacrifice my parents had to make to file for Valin, so he could travel to the states.

It all could've come to a screeching holt if the customs agent found any reason not to allow him to travel on the plane.

The flight went on without a hitch, and of course we all slept the entire flight.

Before long, we landed in John F. Kennedy Airport in New York city. The extraction was a success, there were no issues with customs and the flight departed and landed safely.

My father waited for us in the lobby of the airport and

surprisingly he didn't have to wait too long for us to clear customs. The meet and greet between my father and Valin were memorable.

My father left Jamaica in 1972 when Valin was 6 years old, and that day was the second time since then they saw each other.

They both embraced each other for a while before my father said, "Cum man, we have to go, mi double park, an mi nuh waan no ticket."

He leaned in towards my mother and kissed her on the lips.

Then he took his hand and put it on the top of my head and shook it gently and asked, "Yuh aright?"

I shook my head up and down with his hand was still on top of it.

We carried out our own luggage from the airport lobby into my father's 1982 navy blue Oldsmobile Cutlass supreme sedan.

My father drove back home from the airport to the Bronx. During the drive my parents and Valin was engaged in a deep conversation amongst themselves. My forehead was pressed up against the window of the moving car traveling down the FDR Drive. I couldn't help but reflect on the trip to Jamaica.

I thought that the disparaging remarks that were said about me, would have hurt me deeply, but surprisingly it didn't. I was more perplexed at the notion that I was being ridiculed because I was foreign born. It didn't matter to me that I was a Fatty boom–boom, in their eyes. What concerned me was that their inherent disdain for me stemmed from me being different.

My parents always called me a "Yankee," that meant that it

didn't matter how much I thought I was like them. I could never be a Jamaican. That fact hurt me more than anything anyone ever said about my height, my hair, or weight.

The underlying problem was that I was an outsider who didn't belong to the Jamaican community, nor did I belong with the American or Yankee community. I'm in a class by myself; I'm a born "Jamerican."

One pair

In nature, most things come in pairs,
from lions and lionesses to stallions and mares.
In humans, our karyotype comes in 23 pairs.
With each gender, our chromosomes differ
but connect like zippers, ladders, or stairs–
to renew the circle of life in future years.

The duality in the universe is cause and effect.
We all live to die for us to resurrect.

With the aid of birds and the bees,
seeds planted in fertile soil grow into trees to bear fruit.

The creator of the universe hears
our cries to be alive–our existence rings truth.

[Mark 10:6-9]
[6] From the beginning of creation,
God made them male and female to serve each other.
[7] For this, cause shall a man cleave to his wife
and leave his father and mother.
[8] They twain shall be one flesh: so then they are no more twain,
but one flesh to one another.
[9] What therefore God hath joined together,
let not man put asunder.

Coming to terms with being alone is the sum of all fears.

But finding a suitable mate is like playing musical chairs.
Let us all raise our glasses for this toast, then say, "Cheers!"
With strength, guidance, and perseverance,
both of you stayed together like shears.
The means justify the ends with your venture after all these years.

This journey down the path that the
Almighty prepared cannot be compared.
The Most High has blessed this union
in holy matrimony with care.

Because your time vested in this endeavor
has yielded interest for your heirs,
those dividends have expounded exponentially
like capital gains off shares.

In the relationship, to keep the fire kindling,
more than just mind, body, and soul must be declared.
Being consistent, putting in the effort,
and constantly showing love is rare.

I pray that you both live out the rest of your life –as one pair.

Author's Biography

James Dale is a Jamaican American author. He co-authored **WRITTEN IN VAMPIRE'S BLOOD: THE STRANGER** and wrote **BOUND BY HONOR, BETRAYED BY TRUST**. He also self-published another book of poetry titled: **JUST ANOTHER HOPE-FULL FOOL IN LOVE** which he co-authored with his brother Matthew Dale.

He's earning his Bachelor's in Fine Arts Degree in Creative Writing at Full Sail University. When he's not driving around half the city in a city bus, James posts videos of himself reciting poetry on his YouTube channel. In his spare time, he drives his wife of fourteen years and his three daughters up the wall with laughter from his witty banter and dry sense of humor.

James is currently working on the third installment of his first book of poetry, "JUST ANOTHER HOPE-FULL FOOL IN LOVE." titled **THE PEN IS MIGHTIER THAN THE SWORD**, a snippet of it is available on Smashwords.com.

LinkedIn: **http://www.linkedin.com/mwlite/in/james-dale-89593214**

Instagram: **https://www.instagram.com/justanotherhopefullfoolinlove/**
Twitter: **https://mobile.twitter.com/hopefullfool81**
YouTube channel: **https://youtube.com/user/eaton220ify**

About the Author

Made in the USA
Middletown, DE
25 August 2023